TULLY AND THE MIDNIGHT FEAST

Available in the Tales of Tully series

Tully's Life
This heart-warming story follows the journey of Tully from street dog to much-loved family pet, teaching young readers about the importance of kindness, understanding and hope.

Tully Takes Off!
Tully has arrived in her new home with her new grown-up, but she does not like it one bit! When Tully sees an opportunity to go back to her old life on the streets - the only life she has known up to now - she takes it with both paws. With a search underway, it is up to her new grown-up to work out what Tully needs and help get her safely home.

Tully and the Sad Day
Tully has woken up feeling grey and cloudy inside and she does not know what to do. She cannot help her big feeling because she does not know what it is. As her different feelings begin to work together in the wrong way, it is up to Tully's grown-up to help her to understand what she needs.

Go To Sleep Tully!
It is night time and Tully is tired, but she does not want to go to sleep. Her new grown-up knows that Tully is trying every trick she can to avoid going go to bed! With lots of adventures planned and Tully needing her rest, Tully's grown-up needs to find a way to help Tully learn to not be so worried about bedtime.

Tully and the Midnight Feast
Tully is a newly-adopted dog settling in with her new grown-up. Since her arrival, her snacks have started mysteriously disappearing from the cupboard and appearing under her bed, she seems to have forgotten her manners, and there are days when she just cannot stop eating! Tully and her grown-up need to work together to help Tully with her worries about food.

Tully and the Scary Day
Tully has woken up feeling scared. She isn't really sure why, but today feels like a very scary day, and she just wants to hide. Tully's grown-up is thankfully there to help Tully manage her big feelings and see that the day is not so scary after all.

Don't Touch Tully!
Tully is settling in with her new grown-up. She has learned that the new grown-up is a safe person and she enjoys strokes and cuddles with them. Then Tully starts to meet new people, who want to show her how loved she is. Unfortunately, Tully doesn't feel the same about people she does not know and trust. It is up to Tully's grown-up to find a way to help Tully with her big feelings and to be Tully's voice, when she can't use hers.

Tully and the Tummy Ache
Tully has a tummy ache and it's making her feel quite grumpy. She doesn't want to eat or drink, and she can't get comfortable. Her tummy is sore and it's getting worse! Tully is in a toilet muddle. So, Tully and her grown-up work together to sort the muddle out and help Tully to cure her tummy ache.

Tully's Birthday
It's Tully's birthday, and her grown-up has planned a special day for her, but Tully doesn't feel like celebrating. As the day begins to unfold, so do Tully's big feelings. Tully doesn't know what to do about the big feelings, so she does a bad thing. Luckily, Tully's grown-up is there to help her feel better about herself, and enjoy the rest of her birthday.

Listen, Tully!
Tully does not always like to listen, especially when her grown-up is trying to stop her having fun. Tully decides that instead of listening, she can be in charge. But when things start to go wrong, Tully and her grown-up need to work out how Tully can begin to find listening a little bit easier.

Tully and the Makeover
Tully has been having lots of fun playing in the mud, but now her grown-up says she has to have a bath. Oh dear! Tully is not sure she wants one of those. She is feeling a bit nervous about what is going to happen to her, but Tully's grown-up shows her that there is nothing to worry about. Having a bath is a good thing after all.

Tully and Vera
Tully has moved in with her new grown-up but she is missing her foster carer, Vera. Tully is struggling to understand why she had to leave, and whether it is okay to have big feelings about Vera. It is up to Tully's grown-up to try and help her to understand loss and endings and why, sometimes, they have to happen to make space for new beginnings.

Tully and the Chase
Tully loves to be chased. It gives her a feeling of excitement which starts off as being fun, but one day the excited feeling suddenly and very quickly becomes a feeling which is too big. Instead of feeling excited, Tully starts to feel scared. Tully and her grown-up need to work out how they can play Tully's exciting game without it becoming a bit too much for her, and causing a muddle.

Tully at Christmas
Things are starting to feel a bit different in Tully's house and all around outside. Tully's grown-up looks different, strange lights are appearing everywhere and people have started putting their gardens indoors! Tully is not sure what to make of this thing called Christmas – she just wants everything to stay the same. What can Tully's grown-up do to make Christmas-time a nicer time for both of them?

Tully Goes on Holiday
Tully has gone on a holiday with her grown-up. After a difficult start, things seem to be going well. But when the fairground opens up, with all its flashing lights, loud music and food smells, Tully's big feelings get the better of her, making her want to run. And she does! Tully's grown-up needs to find her in time to show her that holidays can be fun after all.

Tully and the New Rules
Tully likes lots of things about living in a house with her grown-up, but one thing she really doesn't like is all the rules! Tully thinks the rules are all very boring and her grown-up must want to stop her from having fun. One day Tully breaks her least favourite rule, and something bad happens. Tully doesn't know what to do! Can Tully's grown-up get to the bottom of this muddle so it doesn't happen again?

Tully and the Midnight Feast

TALES OF TULLY

Jess van der Hoech

Trauma Tools
& Training

Acknowledgements

As always, to my trusted editor Sarah Ogden for all that you do to make these books come to life. I will never fully know what goes on behind the scenes, but it is a joy to work alongside you on these projects. Thank you.

Thank you to my supervisor Linda Hoggan for your continued support, encouragement, discussion and much-welcomed feedback on this series. I learn so much from you and the knowledge I have gained form our conversations has been invaluable across my practice, the books and now this series. Thank you.

Thank you to Laura Benham, for your support in giving me feedback, the searching questions, your friendship and of course, the countless conversations about dogs, the content of which has become quite useful! Thank you.

To the children and families who I meet in my therapy room, from whom I have learned more about hope and healing than any course could ever teach me. Your input, ideas, questions and answers are so valuable to me and I will be forever grateful. Thank you.

Preface

The *Tales of Tully* Series is based on the adoption of an ex street dog from Bosnia who came to live with me in September 2023. Watching her try to settle and adapt from everything she had previously known to fit in with a new way of life began to present a number of ideas as to how to communicate such difficulties that can be experienced, to others who are in the process of adopting or who have adopted children. The aim of the series is to provide an opportunity to explore different situations, circumstances, feelings and experiences; finding new ways of communicating and understanding each other, through the voice of Tully.

For children who have experienced early trauma, food can be a big issue. It may be that the child is unable to feel their body and recognise hunger or when they are full. Over-eating or under-eating can become a cause for concern. Taking food without asking and hoarding it, or eating all the treats in sight immediately upon arrival to the cupboards, can become a regular behaviour.

Children who have experienced early trauma, and therefore live in a state of stress, can have high levels of the stress hormone cortisol in their bodies. This can cause frequent and strong cravings for sugar, which will release the counteractive hormone dopamine to balance the cortisol. It is not unusual for children who have been traumatised to seek sugar frequently, and this does not always go down well with the parent who wants the child to have safe, healthy foods.

For the child who has been hungry in the past, the fear of not having food is a very real one. The child needs to know and trust that food will always be made available for them and as such, using food as part of behaviour modification for these children is not recommended. Introducing snack boxes that the child has access to can be helpful, with the contents and how often they will be replenished assisting parents to help the child to understand boundaries, future thinking and natural consequences. For example, if the snacks are to last until Friday but they are eaten by Wednesday, there will be no more snacks in the snack box, but there will be snacks available in the kitchen, that may be a bit more boring!

When Tully first came to the UK, having previously had to survive as a street dog in Bosnia, she would sometimes wait for hours to eat her food. I began leaving her food out for her all day, but quickly realised that this was counter-intuitive as I was trying to create healthy routines for her. She soon learned that food would be produced in the morning and evening, a suitable meal plan for a dog. When I gave her food that she really liked, she would eat it immediately, whereas the less preferred flavours she could leave. High value treats were stashed in her bed, until she realised that this food would be available to her all the time.

Similarly, I have noted in my therapy room that food can be an issue in families, which becomes quite a tricky experience given that eating is a daily occurrence. As children become more aware of a feeling of safety, not previously experienced, and of the physical signals and information provided by their own bodies in relation to hunger and other feelings, issues around food begin to be addressed in a positive way at home.

How to use this book

First and foremost, ensure that both you and the child are well-regulated and comfortable when you begin to read Tully's story. Make sure you choose a time when you are unlikely to be interrupted. The child may like a soother, a favourite or fidget toy, a drink or something to suck or chew to help them to stay regulated.

If the child is calm, then begins to try and distract or move away from the reading, make a note of what they have just heard in the text. It is very likely that they will have just provided you with some valuable information about something that they cannot tolerate or want to avoid for now.

The questions have been designed not only to explore the internal world of the child, but to help to develop a common language between the child and adult who are using this book together. The child cannot get the answers to the questions incorrect. Their interpretation of the thoughts and feelings Tully is having may provide some very significant information about the child's own thoughts and feelings. The child may want to expand the answers to talk about themselves and may even be able to make comparisons between Tully's feelings and their own.

Tully and the Midnight Feast

"Good morning Tully, it's a beautiful day!"

Tully woke up and stretched. She went to see her grown up for her morning chin scratch. Today would be a good day.

Can you draw Tully?

Tully's grown-up was looking in the cupboard. The grown-up had found an empty packet of dog treats.

"I thought there were some in here," the grown-up said. "Do you know where they are?"

Tully looked at her grown-up innocently.

What might have happened to the dog treats?

Tully knew where the treats were. She had sneaked into the cupboard in the middle of the night and taken the treats, but she had not eaten them.

Tully had hidden the treats in her dog bed very carefully.

They weren't the only treats in her bed; Tully had been collecting and hiding treats for a while now. She had lots.

Why might Tully be hiding the treats?

Why has she chosen to hide them in her bed?

When Tully had been a puppy, she had lived as a street dog in Bosnia.

Tully had had to find her own food. Sometimes a kind lady had come to feed her, but Tully had not always been able to stay in the same place, and the lady couldn't always find her to feed her. So sometimes Tully would go hungry.

Tully had gotten used to hiding food when she was on the streets, to save it for the days when she could not find any. Tully did not want to have that hungry feeling again.

Why might Tully think she will have the hungry feeling again?

Where do you feel a hungry feeling in your body?

Tully's grown-up always made sure that there was enough food for Tully, but Tully still wanted to hide some.

"What is that horrible smell?" Tully's grown-up said, looking around Tully's bed.

Uh oh! Tully's grown up had found Tully's secret stash of treats! Some of them had been under Tully's bed for so long, they had gone mouldy and were now making Tully's bed smell bad. Yuck!

Does Tully mind that the treats are making her bed smell?

Tully knew her grown-up had found her sneaky stash from her midnight feasts. It gave her a big feeling.

Tully's grown-up cleaned up the mouldy food and threw it away.

"I'm sorry Tully, this has got to go," the grown-up said and put the food in the bin.

Why didn't the grown-up want Tully to eat the food?

How does Tully feel now that the food is in the bin?

What plan might Tully make now?

At dinner time, when Tully's meal was placed in front of her she ate it all up in three big mouthfuls.

"Where are your manners, Tully?!" the grown-up said.

Tully went looking for more food. She didn't feel full up at all.

Why might Tully not be feeling full up today?

Tully saw her grown-up's meal on the kitchen counter. She knew she shouldn't, but she jumped up and snatched the food from her grown up's plate.

Tully was starting to get big feelings. She had been caught with the treats she had taken without asking, upset her grown-up by not having good manners at dinner, and now she had eaten her grown-up's meal.

What feelings might Tully have?

Tully went outside to see if she could find an old bone she might have buried in the garden. She was still hungry.

As she was digging a hole, her grown-up called her in to the house. There was a box next to her bed that Tully had not seen before. It had some treats in it.

"Tully, this is your snack box," her grown-up said, "This is where your treats can go so they don't go mouldy underneath your bed. I know there have been times when you were hungry, but I want you to know you will always have food here. You don't need to eat mine either!" her grown-up said, tickling Tully's ears.

"I think you've got some really big feelings that don't feel so good and when you get big feelings, it can switch on your good feelings tummy. Your hungry tummy is full, but your good feelings tummy still feels empty. So you try to fill it up with food. But too much food is not healthy and you'll get a tummy ache."

What do you think Tully's good feelings tummy needs?

"When you need your good feelings tummy to be filled, you can come and see me for a cuddle or a game. We could go for a walk and a sniff because you love that. You could remember all of the good words about yourself. You can think about how you are safe now and I will always keep you safe."

What else could Tully do to help her to feel the good feelings?

Tully always had snacks in her snack box and because her grown-up knew where the snacks were, the grown-up could make sure they were always tasty and fresh. Tully began to notice the difference between her feelings tummy and her hungry tummy.

Tully and her grown-up worked together to help Tully with the feelings that made her feel good. Tully knows that she is safe now.

What good feelings words do you know about yourself?

Who are the people who can help you to find the good words about yourself?

Jess van der Hoech

About the author

Jess van der Hoech is a qualified therapist who has spent the last ten years studying and working with the impact of developmental trauma and, in particular, the assessment and treatment of children and adolescents with complex trauma and dissociation.

As well as supporting birth families, Jess works with looked-after and adopted children and families, using skills in attachment-focused therapy and therapeutic parenting techniques.

Jess is a supervisor, trainer and motivational speaker with a passion for writing therapeutic books that are accessible to children and families to help with the healing process and to increase awareness in the impact of trauma.

Jess van der Hoech

Also by Jess van der Hoech

What A Muddle (2016) ISBN 978 18381987 0 1 (Co-authored with Renée Potgieter Marks)
An interactive, practical workbook designed to help children who have difficulties with emotional regulation to begin to understand what is happening in their bodies. A variety of activities throughout the book enable the child to start to explore these ideas through the story of Sam, while gently encouraging them to begin to verbalise their own experiences. Carrying out the physical exercises in the book can promote changes in emotional regulation. The text is written in a child-friendly, gender-neutral style, and is easy to understand for parents, carers and practitioners alike. For children aged 4-12.

These Three Words (2018) ISBN 978 18381987 5 6
Also available as an e-book. A unique therapeutic novel for teenagers with the aim of linking together the feelings, emotions and behaviours connected to anxiety, with some of the therapeutic tools that can be used in order to enable better self-regulation, increased confidence and different ways of thinking. The book is equally valuable to parents of teenagers with anxiety, giving them an insight and understanding into some of the issues that may be affecting their child, and potentially opening up a line of communication and a way forward between parent and teen.

These Three Words: The Journal (2019) ISBN 978 18381987 2 5
A thought-provoking and hands-on workbook, combining a series of practical exercises and tools designed to assist teenagers who are struggling with the symptoms of anxiety. Addressing the anxious responses in both brain and body, this journal provides the reader with the opportunity to discover therapeutic coping techniques and learn how to apply them to their own personal problem areas, before committing to a twenty-eight-day practice to promote good emotional regulation and reduced anxiety. The journal can be used alongside the therapeutic novel These Three Words, or as a standalone workbook, and it is suitable for use by the teenage reader on their own, with a parent, or in a group.

Beastie, Baby and the Brand-New Mummy (2022) ISBN 978 18381987 3 2 and *Beastie, Baby and the Brand-New Daddy (2022) ISBN 978 18381987 4 9*
A therapeutic story that looks at the external signs of pathological dissociation in a child. Dolly's story helps children who have experienced early trauma to begin to understand, in a very simple way, what dissociation is and why it has happened in their internal world. Tools and techniques are included within the story that parents and caregivers can use to assist the child in the first stages of their healing process. Beautiful illustrations on every page enhance the story of Dolly, and help the reader to relate to the events that happen, to notice the methods Dolly has developed to manage her feelings, and to think about what is happening in their own internal world. For children aged 4-12

Printed in Great Britain
by Amazon

62815082R00020